Georgetown Elementary School
Indian Prairie School District
Aurora, Illinois

TABLE OF
CONTENTS

HOW TO USE THIS DICTIONARY

This book is full of useful phrases in both English and French. The English phrase appears first, followed by the French phrase. Look below each French phrase for help to sound it out. Try reading the phrases aloud.

Topic heading in English

Topic heading in French

Additional phrases to learn

Phrase in English
Phrase in French
(pronunciation)

NOTES ABOUT THE FRENCH LANGUAGE

Nouns in French are masculine or feminine. The French words for "a," "an," "the," and "some" tell a noun's gender. Here is a quick reference guide:

English word	Masculine	Feminine	Plural
a/an	un	une	des
the	le	la	les
some	du	de la	des

The forms of many adjectives change to match the noun. For example, the word "happy" is written as "heureux" if the speaker is male and "heureuse" if the speaker is female.

In this phrase book, the phrases match the gender of the characters shown on each page.

3

LETTERS OF THE ALPHABET
AND THEIR PRONUNCIATIONS

A a • ah

B b • bay

C c • say

D d • day

E e • uh

F f • eff

G g • zhay

H h • AH-sh

I i • ee

J j • zhee

K k • ka

L l • ell

M m • emm

N n • enn

O o • oh

P p • pay

Q q • koo

R r • air

S s • ess

T t • tay

U u • ew

V v • vay

W w • doo-BLUH vay

X x • gz

Y y • ee

Z z • zz

IT SOUNDS LIKE

There are 26 letters in the French alphabet. These letters include the same letters as the English alphabet. Most of these letters sound the same. But there are some letters and letter combinations in French that sound different. You can use this guide to learn how to say these sounds. In addition, some words have silent letters. These letters appear at the end of a word. Look at the pronunciations for help to sound out these words.

	SOUND	PRONUNCIATION	EXAMPLES	
CONSONANTS	c	if followed by a, o, or u like c in cat; if followed by e, i, or y, like s in seat	cartable	KAR-ta-bluh
			cigale	SEE-gahl
	ch	like sh in chef	chat	shah
	ç	like s in seat	français	frahn-SAY
	gn	like ny in canyon	espagnol	es-PAH-nyol
	h	h is silent	haricot	AH-ri-coh
	j and sometimes g	like s in measure	jambe	ZHAM-buh
	ll	like l in mill or y in yes	belle	bell
			famille	fa-MEE-yeh
	qu	like k in kitten	bibliothèque	bib-lee-o-TEK
	w	like v in very	wagon	va-GOHN
	x	silent at the end of a word except in six and dix where it sounds like s; like gz in exit if in the middle of a word	dix	deece
			examen	eg-ZA-ma
	y	like ee in sheep	y	ee
VOWELS	a, à, â	like a in cat	paté	pah-TAY
	e	like uh in hungry	arbre	ar-BRUH
	é	like ay in may	téléphone	tay-lay-FONE
	è	like e in set or a in mare	zèbre	zeb-BRUH
			père	pare
	ê	like e in met	tête	tett
	i	like e in me	lit	lee
	o	like o in hole	mot	moh
	u	like ew in dew	rue	rew
VOWEL COMBINATIONS	au	like o in hole	auto	OH-to
	ai	like ay in day	maison	MAY-sohn
	oi	like wha in what	roi	rwha
	ou	like oo in loop	genou	zhuh-NOO
	œ	The sound "oe" can change with each word. Look at the pronunciation for help.		

French: LES BASES (lay baahs)

Thank you.
Merci.
(mer-SEE)

You are welcome.
De rien.
(duh REE-un)

What is your name?
Quel est ton nom?
(kel ay tohn nohn)

My name is___.
Mon nom est___.
(mohn nohn ay___)

MORE TO LEARN

Yes	No
Oui	**Non**
(wee)	(nohn)

I live in an apartment.
J'habite dans un appartement.
(zah-BEET dahn uhn a-parte-UH-mahn)

Where do you live?
Où habites-tu?
(oo abeet tew)

a house
une maison
(oon MAY-sohn)

My address is ___.
Mon adresse est ____.
(mohn AD-ress ay ___)

MORE TO LEARN

My phone number is ___.
Mon numéro de téléphone est ____.
(mohn nu-MAY-roh duh tay-lay-FONE ay___)
See page 30 for numbers.

English: MEALS

Are you hungry?
As-tu faim?
(ah tew fuhn)

I am hungry.
J'ai faim.
(zay fam)

thirsty
soif
(swaf)

What is for supper?
Qu'est-ce qu'il y a pour le dîner?
(kay suh keel ee ah poor luh dee-NAY)

lunch
le déjeuner
(luh day-ZHUH-nay)

breakfast
le petit-déjeuner
(luh PUH-tee day-ZHUH-nay)

MORE TO LEARN

I am not hungry.
Je n'ai pas faim.
(zhuh nay pah fam)

12

French: **REPAS** (RUH-pah)

Can we go out to eat?
Pouvons-nous sortir pour aller manger?
(POO-voun noo sor-TEER poor ah-LAY mahn-ZHAY)

I like Chinese food.
J'aime la nourriture chinoise.
(zaym lah noo-REE-tewr SHEEN-waz)

I don't like strawberry ice cream.
Je n'aime pas la glace à la fraise.
(zhuh naym pah lah glass ah lah frehz)

CHINESE

13

French: **FAMILLE** (fah-MEE-ye)

Do you speak English?
Parlez-vous anglais?
(PAR-lay voo ahn-GLAY)

French
français
(frahn-SAY)

German
allemand
(a-LUH-mahn)

Spanish
espagnol
(es-pah-NYOL)

Chinese
chinois
(SHEEN-wa)

A little.
Un peu.
(uhn puh)

DUTY FREE

7 8 9 10 11

MORE TO LEARN

father
père
(pare)

sister
sœur
(sur)

brother
frère
(frare)

It is time to get up.
Il est l'heure de se lever.
(eel ay luhr deuh suh le-VAY)

What time is it?
Quelle heure est-il?
(kel uhr ay teel)

It is time to go to bed.
Il est l'heure d'aller au lit.
(eel ay luhr DAH-lay oh lee)

When are we leaving?
Quand partons-nous?
(kahn par-TOHN noo)

French: DATES ET TEMPS (daht ay tahn)

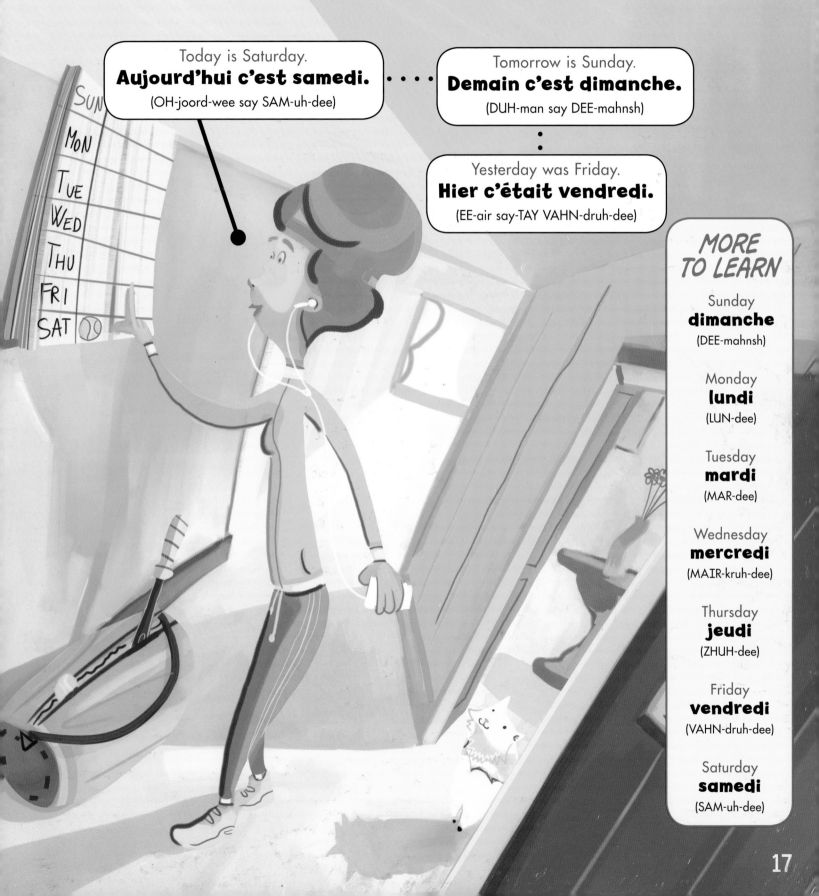

Today is Saturday.
Aujourd'hui c'est samedi.
(OH-joord-wee say SAM-uh-dee)

Tomorrow is Sunday.
Demain c'est dimanche.
(DUH-man say DEE-mahnsh)

Yesterday was Friday.
Hier c'était vendredi.
(EE-air say-TAY VAHN-druh-dee)

MORE TO LEARN

Sunday
dimanche
(DEE-mahnsh)

Monday
lundi
(LUN-dee)

Tuesday
mardi
(MAR-dee)

Wednesday
mercredi
(MAIR-kruh-dee)

Thursday
jeudi
(ZHUH-dee)

Friday
vendredi
(VAHN-druh-dee)

Saturday
samedi
(SAM-uh-dee)

Happy birthday!
Joyeux anniversaire!
(jwa-YEUHZ ann-ee-VAIR-sair)

When is your birthday?
Quand est ton anniversaire?
(kan ay tohn ann-ee-VAIR-sair)

My birthday is in May.
Mon anniversaire est en mai.
(mohn ann-ee-VAIR-sair ay tahn may)

French: MOIS ET SAISONS (mwa ay SAY-sohn)

I love summer!
J'aime l'été!
(zaym LAY-tay)

fall
l'automne
(LO-tonne)

winter
l'hiver
(LEE-ver)

spring
le printemps
(luh PRIHN-tahn)

MORE TO LEARN

January
janvier
(ZA-nvee-ay)

February
février
(FAY-vree-ay)

March
mars
(mars)

April
avril
(AV-reel)

May
mai
(may)

June
juin
(JU-an)

July
juillet
(JWEE-yay)

August
août
(oot)

September
septembre
(SEP-tahm-bruh)

October
octobre
(OK-toh-bruh)

November
novembre
(NO-vahm-bruh)

December
décembre
(DAY-sahm-bruh)

French: **LE TEMPS** (luh tahn)

It is <u>cold</u>.
Il fait froid.
(eel fay frwa)

hot
chaud
(show)

Wear a coat.
Mets un manteau.
(may uhn MAHN-toh)

hat
un chapeau
(uhn SHA-poh)

mittens
des moufles
(day MOO-fle)

boots
des bottes
(day bott)

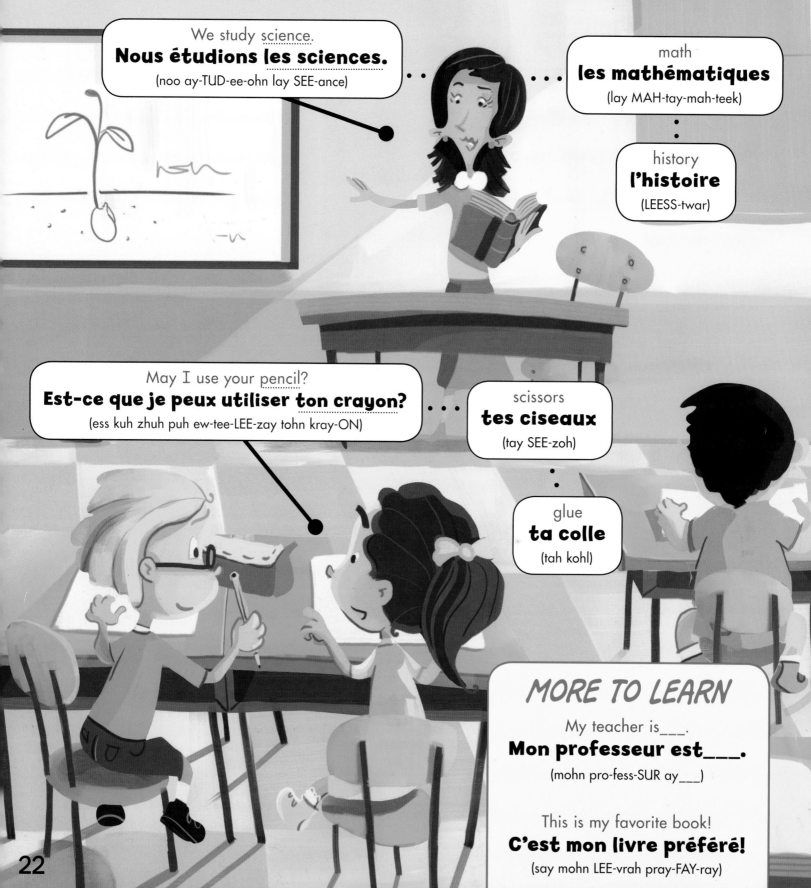

We study science.
Nous étudions les sciences.
(noo ay-TUD-ee-ohn lay SEE-ance)

math
les mathématiques
(lay MAH-tay-mah-teek)

history
l'histoire
(LEESS-twar)

May I use your pencil?
Est-ce que je peux utiliser ton crayon?
(ess kuh zhuh puh ew-tee-LEE-zay tohn kray-ON)

scissors
tes ciseaux
(tay SEE-zoh)

glue
ta colle
(tah kohl)

MORE TO LEARN

My teacher is___.
Mon professeur est___.
(mohn pro-fess-SUR ay___)

This is my favorite book!
C'est mon livre préféré!
(say mohn LEE-vrah pray-FAY-ray)

French: **L'ÉCOLE** (lay kohl)

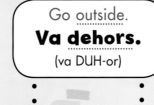

Numbers • LES CHIFFRES (lay SHEE-freh)

1 one • **un**
(un)

2 two • **deux**
(duh)

3 three • **trois**
(twah)

4 four • **quatre**
(KAT-trah)

5 five • **cinq**
(sank)

6 six • **six**
(seece)

7 seven • **sept**
(set)

8 eight • **huit**
(weet)

9 nine • **neuf**
(neuf)

10 ten • **dix**
(deese)

11 eleven • **onze**
(onz)

12 twelve • **douze**
(dooz)

13 thirteen • **treize**
(trez)

14 fourteen • **quatorze**
(KAT-orz)

15 fifteen • **quinze**
(kanz)

16 sixteen • **seize**
(sez)

17 seventeen • **dix-sept**
(deese-SET)

18 eighteen • **dix-huit**
(deese-WEET)

19 nineteen • **dix-neuf**
(deese-NEUF)

20 twenty • **vingt**
(van)

30 thirty • **trente**
(trahnt)

40 forty • **quarante**
(KA-rant)

50 fifty • **cinquante**
(SANK-ant)

60 sixty • **soixante**
(SWA-sant)

70 seventy • **soixante-dix**
(SWA-sant deese)

80 eighty • **quatre-vingt**
(KAT-trah van)

90 ninety •
quatre-vingt-dix
(KAT-trah van deese)

100 one hundred • **cent**
(sahn)

Colors • LES COULEURS (lay cool-UR)

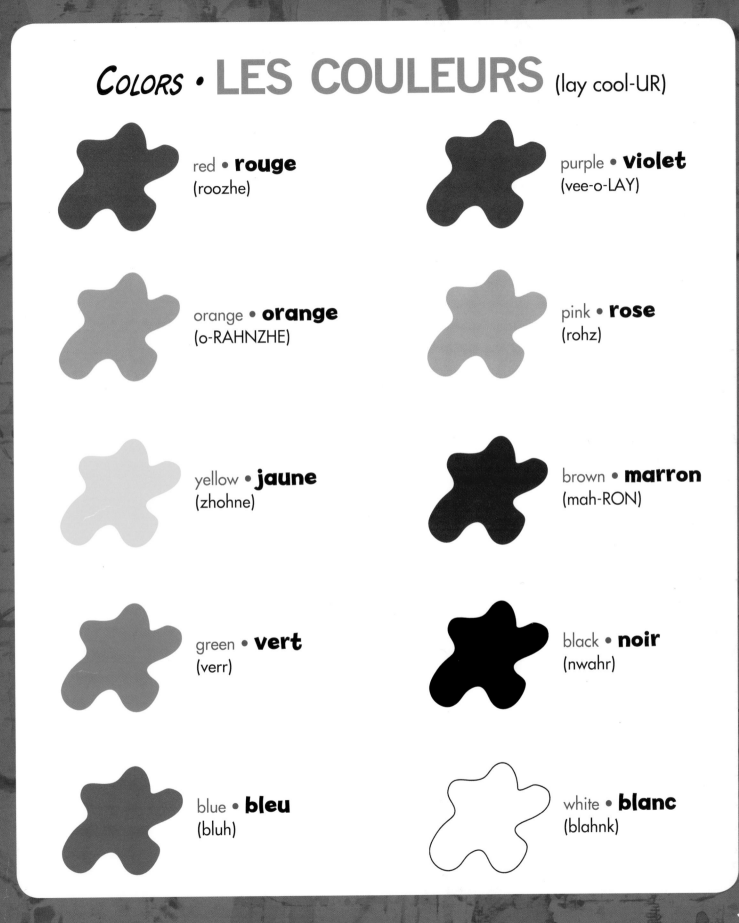

red • **rouge**
(roozhe)

purple • **violet**
(vee-o-LAY)

orange • **orange**
(o-RAHNZHE)

pink • **rose**
(rohz)

yellow • **jaune**
(zhohne)

brown • **marron**
(mah-RON)

green • **vert**
(verr)

black • **noir**
(nwahr)

blue • **bleu**
(bluh)

white • **blanc**
(blahnk)

31

READ MORE

Demarest, Chris L. *My House: Lift-the-Flap Board Book = Ma maison livre anime.* Singapore: Berlitz Pub./Apa Publications, 2007.

Kudela, Katy R. *My First Book of French Words.* Bilingual Picture Dictionaries. Mankato, Minn.: Capstone Press, 2010.

Stanley, Mandy. *My First French Book.* New York: Kingfisher, 2007.

INTERNET SITES

FactHound offers a safe, fun way to find Internet sites related to this book. All of the sites on FactHound have been researched by our staff.

Here's all you do:

Visit *www.facthound.com*

Type in this code: 9781404871533

Super-cool stuff! Check out projects, games and lots more at **www.capstonekids.com**

LOOK FOR ALL THE BOOKS IN THE SPEAK ANOTHER LANGUAGE! SERIES:

MY FIRST FRENCH *PHRASES*

MY FIRST GERMAN *PHRASES*

MY FIRST MANDARIN CHINESE *PHRASES*

MY FIRST SPANISH *PHRASES*

Editor: Katy Kudela
Designer: Alison Thiele
Art Director: Nathan Gassman
Production Specialist: Danielle Ceminsky
The illustrations in this book were created digitally.

Picture Window Books
1710 Roe Crest Drive
North Mankato, MN 56003
www.capstonepub.com

Library of Congress Cataloging-in-Publication Data
Kalz, Jill.
  My first French phrases / by Jill Kalz; illustrated by Danielle Fabbri.
    p. cm.—(Speak another language)
  Includes bibliographical references.
  Summary: "Simple text paired with themed illustrations invite the reader to learn to speak French"—Provided by publisher.
  ISBN 978-1-4048-7153-3 (library binding)
  ISBN 978-1-4048-7244-8 (paperback)
  1. French language—Textbooks for foreign speakers—English—Juvenile literature. I. Title.
  PC2445.K25 2012
  448.3'421—dc23   2011027196

Printed in the United States of America in North Mankato, Minnesota.
112012   006976R